Amazing Bible Stories

7 Stories from the Old Testament

Music ON OFF

Zonderkidz

CREATION
GENESIS 1

DAY 1

In the beginning, God created the heavens and the earth. He said, "Let there be light," and there was light.

Then God said, "Let there be a huge space between the waters." God called this space "sky."

DAY 2

DAY 3

Next God said, "Let dry ground appear, and let the land grow plants."

After that, God made the sun to shine during the day. He made the moon to light up the night.

DAY 4

The next day, God said, "Let the waters be filled with living things, and let birds fly in the sky."

DAY 5

Then God said, "Let the land **produce** living creatures." He made animals and Adam and Eve.

DAY 6

Finally, God saw that everything he had made was good! So he rested.

DAY 7

Message For Me

game

repeat

3

ADAM & EVE
GENESIS 2-3

GO

God planted a garden in **Eden** and filled it with all kinds of flowers, plants, trees and animals. Adam's job was to name all the animals and to care for the garden.

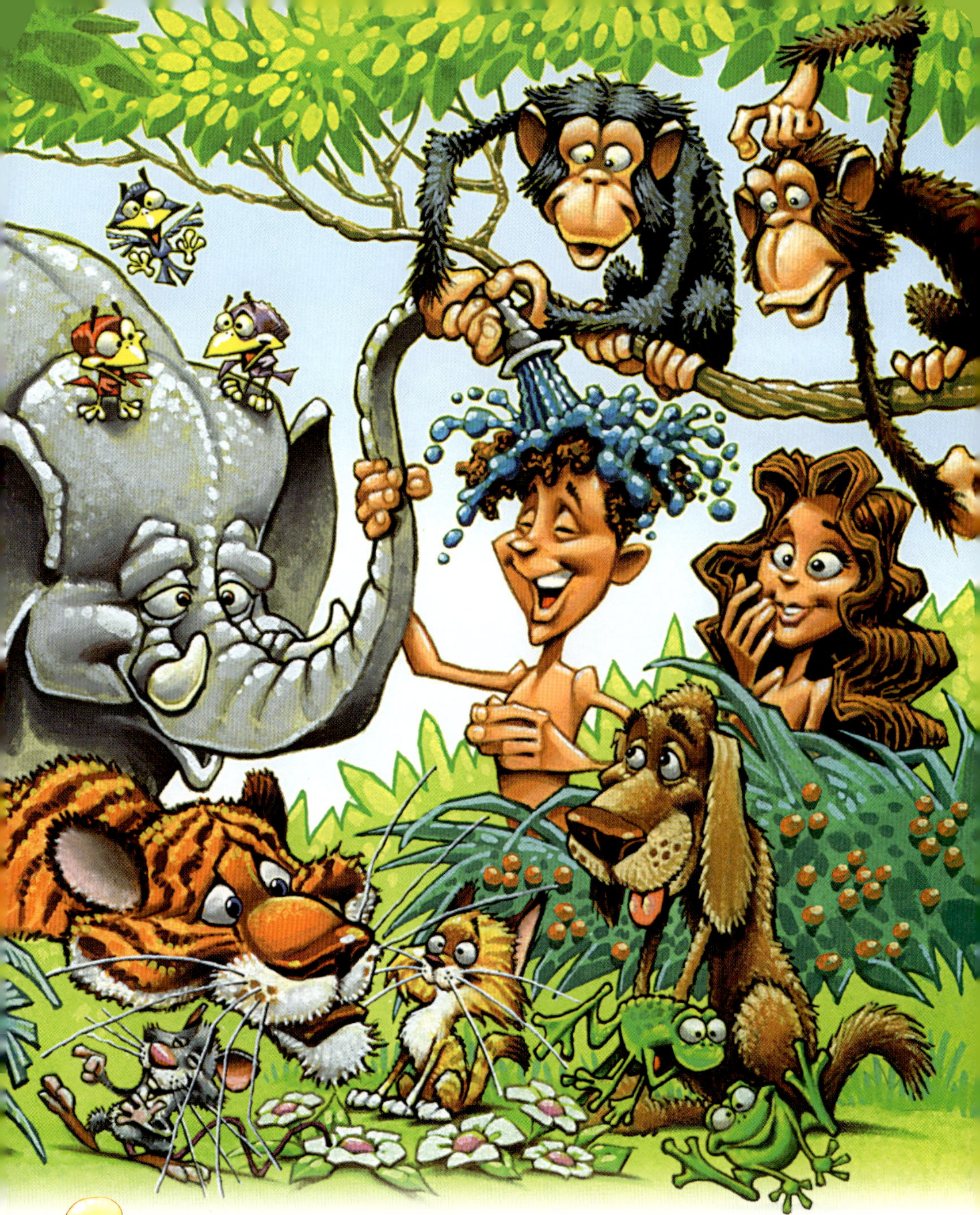

 God didn't want Adam to be lonely, so he made a wife for him. God made Adam fall asleep, and then he took one of Adam's ribs and created Eve.

Adam and Eve were very happy living in the garden. God gave them one important rule: "You can eat the fruit of any tree except the tree of knowledge of good and evil."

One day, a sly serpent told Eve to eat the **forbidden** fruit. "You will be as wise as God," the serpent hissed. "You will be powerful." Eve took the fruit and ate it. She gave some to Adam and he ate it too.

Think About It

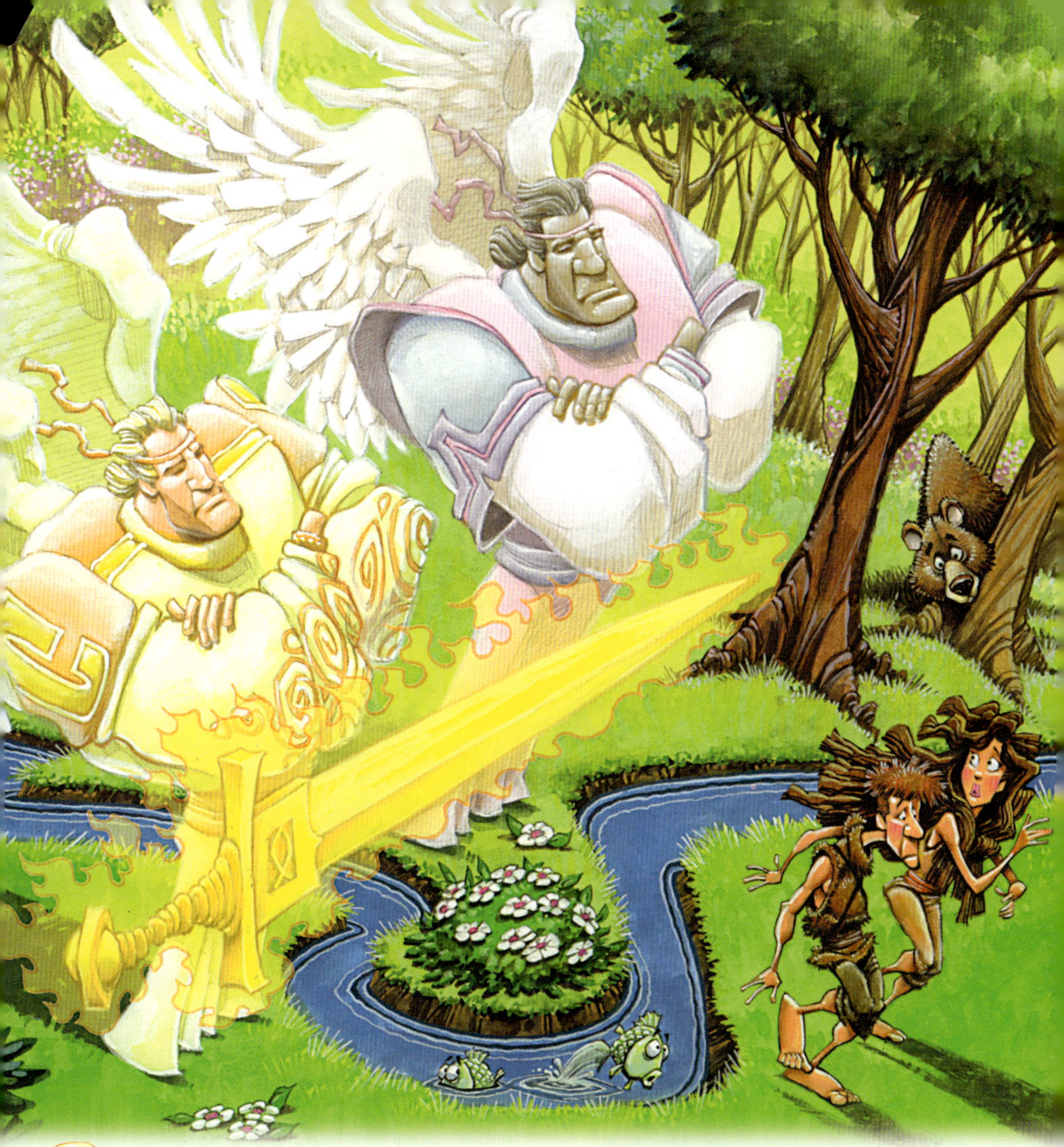

God knew that Adam and Eve had **disobeyed** him, so he made them leave the garden. God placed two angels in front of the garden with a flaming sword to make sure Adam and Eve could not return. But God still loved them.

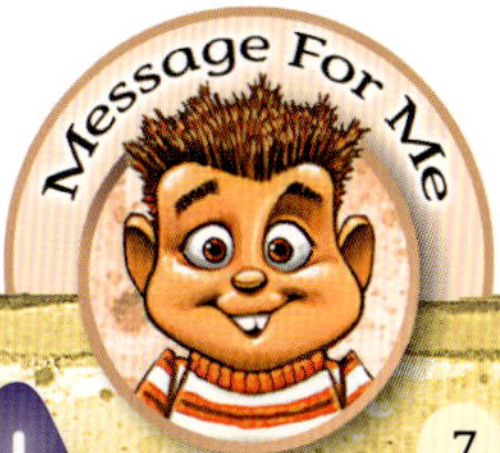

NOAH'S ARK
GENESIS 6-8

The people of the earth were being **sinful** and mean. So God decided to send a flood and start over again. But there was one good man – Noah. He followed God's ways.

God said to Noah, "Build an **ark**. Bring a male and a female of every living thing into the ark. Then bring your family, too." Noah did everything exactly as God commanded.

It rained and rained for 40 days and 40 nights. But everyone in the boat was safe and dry.

Finally, the rain stopped and the ark landed on a mountain. Noah sent a dove to search for dry land. The dove returned with an olive leaf in its beak!

STOP

Think About It

Noah and his family and all the animals came out of the ark and celebrated. God sent a rainbow as a sign of his **covenant** to never again send such a flood.

Jacob **adored** his son Joseph. He made Joseph a beautiful robe with many colors. That made Joseph's brothers jealous.

One day, Joseph's brothers took his robe and threw him into a well. Later, they sold Joseph to **traders** who took him to **Egypt**, then told their father that Joseph had been eaten by a wild animal.

In Egypt, Joseph worked hard for the **pharaoh** and became a **governor**. His job was to store all the grain. When **famine** struck the land, Joseph's brothers traveled to Egypt to buy some grain. When they got there, they didn't even recognize Joseph!

Think About It

Joseph tested his brothers to see if they had changed for the better. When he saw that his brothers weren't mean anymore, he cried out, "I am Joseph! I am your brother!"

Joseph's brothers were afraid, because they knew they had been very mean to him. But Joseph **forgave** them!

MOSES
EXODUS 2-34

Pharaoh, the king of Egypt, thought there were too many **Israelite** people in his kingdom. One Israelite woman hid her baby boy in a basket among the reeds of the **Nile River**, to keep him safe.

The baby's sister, Miriam, watched over her brother until Pharaoh's daughter found him. Pharaoh's daughter decided to keep the baby for her own. She called him Moses and raised him in the palace in Egypt.

Years later, Moses saw the Egyptians treating the Israelites badly. So, Moses fled Egypt to work in the fields **tending** sheep. The Israelites cried out to God for help.

One day Moses saw a bush on fire, but it did not burn up. God spoke from inside the burning bush, "Go to Pharaoh and tell him to let my people go. They are **suffering**."

Moses told Pharaoh, "Let the Israelites go. Free them from **slavery**." The pharaoh said, "NO!"

So God sent 10 terrible **plagues** to convince Pharaoh to let the people go. The pharaoh finally said, "GO!"

THE 10 PLAGUES

BLZZZ

Moses led the Israelites through the desert for 40 years to the land God promised them.

CANAAN

N
W — E
S

MOUNT SINAI

SEA

Message For Me

game

repeat

21

GO

After the Israelites entered into the promised land, they had to fight many enemies. Once, before a fight with the Philistine army, a **mighty** soldier named Goliath came down from the Philistine camps. "Who will fight me?" roared 9-foot-tall Goliath.

 David, a young Israelite boy, was bringing food to his brothers and heard Goliath's **dare**.

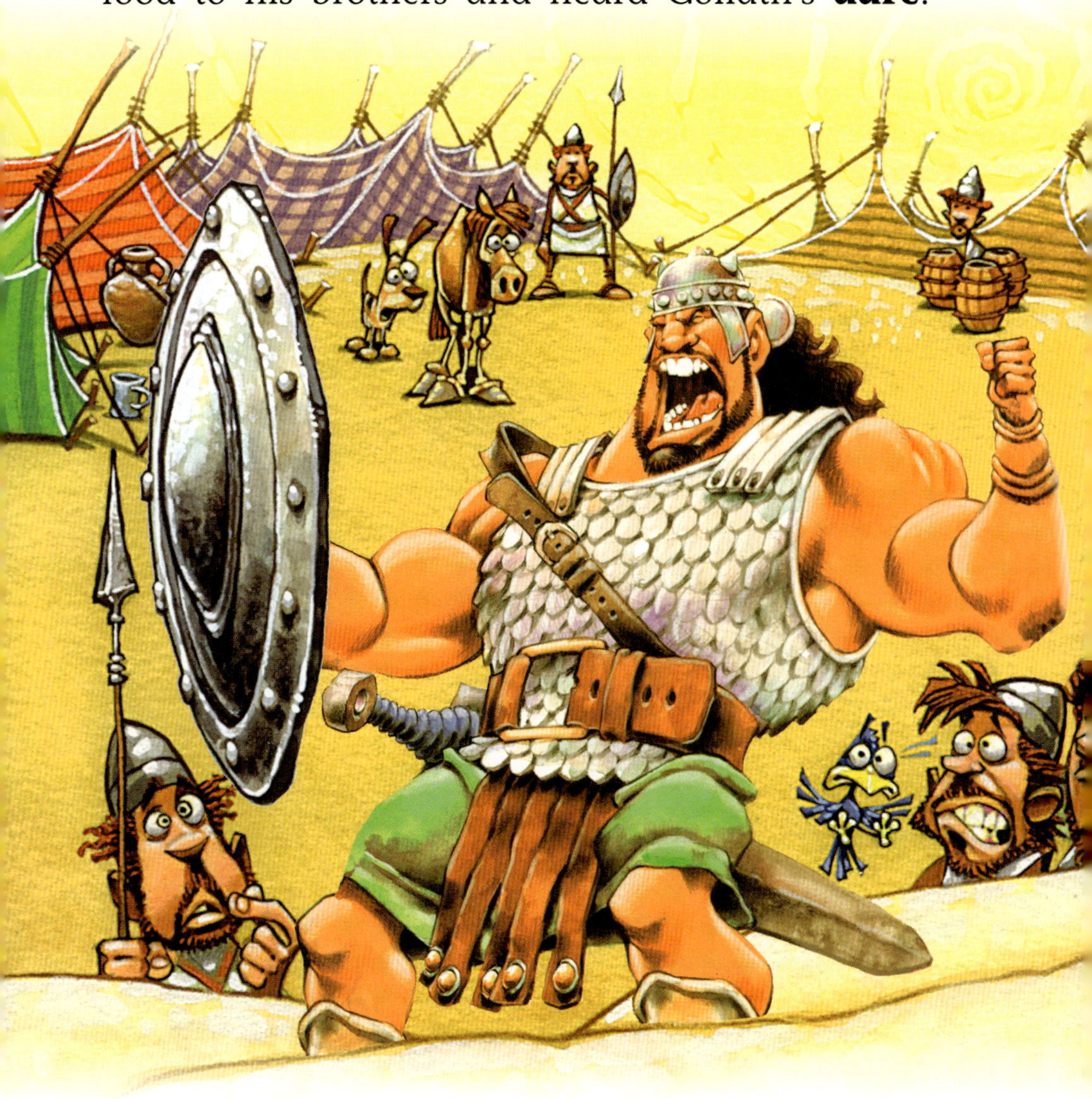

 David said, "I'll fight him." However, **King Saul**, the leader of the Israelite army, believed David was too young. David **convinced** King Saul that with God's help he could fight the giant and win.

David went to a stream and chose five smooth stones. Putting a stone in his sling, he **approached** Goliath and slung the stone at him. It hit Goliath on the forehead, and he fell to the ground with a crash. David had won!

Think About It

JONAH AND THE HUGE FISH
JONAH 1-2

The people of **Nineveh** were sinning and sinning. God sent Jonah to Nineveh to tell the people to stop. Jonah didn't want to go, so he got on a boat and sailed away from Nineveh. God sent a wild storm. The **frightened** sailors asked Jonah what to do.

Think About It

yes

no

game 1

Jonah said, "Throw me into the sea." When they did, the sea became calm. Then God sent a huge fish to swallow Jonah. He was inside the fish for 3 days and 3 nights. He prayed to God, and the fish spit him out. Jonah went to Nineveh and the people listened to him. They stopped sinning and followed God's ways.

Message For Me

Keep your child learning by leaps and bounds with the Never-Ending Learning™ Club!

Activity Sheets Available Online!

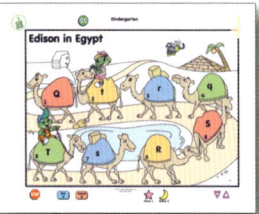

Fun activities like those found in your LeapPad® books are also available online in a convenient 12-month subscription. With a Mind Station® connector, you can print Activity Sheets right at home on your own printer! Yearly subscriptions are available for *Kindergarten & 1st Grade*.

Leap's Pond™ Interactive Magazine

Thrill your child with *Leap's Pond* magazine packed with puzzles, games, stories and activities. Use the Mind Station connector and reusable cartridge to download the dazzling interactive content that makes the magic of *Leap's Pond* magazine come to life. You'll find selections from 6 core curriculum areas in each issue. *Ages 4-7*

The **Mind Station®** connector works with LeapFrog.com to transfer fun and challenging activities to a reusable cartridge. Pop the cartridge in your LeapPad player and bring materials to life!

Purchase a **Mind Station®** connector and join the Never-Ending Learning Club. You'll have access to new activities for all of your Internet-enabled LeapFrog® and Quantum Leap® learning toys.*

* A computer and Internet connection are required

Sign up at www.leapfrog.com and get hours of learning & fun delivered to your door. The Mind Station connector is also available to purchase online, or at your nearest LeapFrog retail partner.